WELCOME FRIENDS

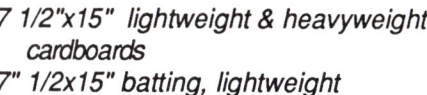

YOU WILL NEED:

7 1/2"x15" lightweight & heavyweight cardboards
7" 1/2x15" batting, lightweight
4"x5" thermolam or needlepunch
8"x15 1/2" fabric for background
2"x16" green fabric (grass)
4"x5" fabric (house)
3"x4" fabric (roof)
2"x3" fabric (chimney)
3"x3" fabric (door & shutters)
1"x1 1/2" white fabric (window)
scraps of lace & trim
14" of 1/16" wide white ribbon
11" of 1/8" wide pink & blue ribbon
2" of 1/8" wide ribbon (hanger)
paint or pens for saying (see introduction)
4 bunches of cloth flowers
6 small artificial leaves
1 white pearl seed bead (doorknob)
1--2" tall sisal tree and 2--1" tall trees
green floral tape
small nail
iron on transfer pencil
craft glue or glue gun

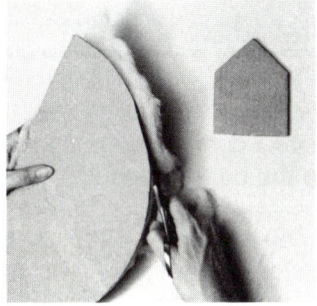
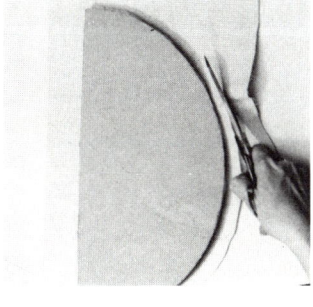
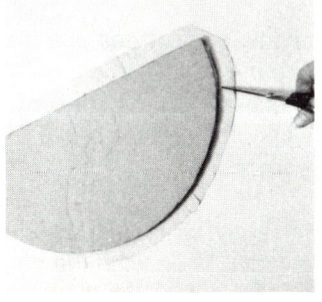

1 Trace the background, house, roofs and chimney patterns on page 3. Cut them out of heavyweight cardboard, be sure to glue the two house patterns together. Glue the batting to the background and trim to fit.

2 Place the background cardboard on the fabric with the batting side against the wrong side of the fabric. Trim so the fabric is 1/2" larger than the cardboard.

3 Cut the corners diagonally 1/4" from the cardboard. Clip the curved edges every 1". Cut to 1/8" from the cardboard.

4 On the wrong side of the background, run a bead of glue around the outside edge. Begin with the corners and pull the fabric onto the cardboard. Do the curved edges next and the straight edge last.

5

6

5. Trace the saying from page 3 onto a piece of plain paper. Turn the paper over and with the transfer pencil, go over the letters. Position the saying on the background and iron to transfer the saying.

6. Use acrylic paints, liquid embroidery or a felt tip pen to make the saying.

7

8

7. For the grass: unravel 1/2" of one long side of the fabric. Glue to the bottom straight edge of the background. Cut out the background shape from lightweight cardboard and glue to the back. Glue the 2" piece of ribbon as shown.

8. For the house: lightly glue the thermolam to the house, trim to fit. Cover with fabric as in step 4. Glue on the window, shutters, door and a bit of lace for the curtain. Attach the lace trims as pictured.

9. Glue down 1/16" wide ribbon to outline the door and window (a syringe-type applicator makes this easy). Glue the bead on for a doorknob. Glue the house to the background.

9

10

10. For the roofs: cover the narrow ends first, then the longer ends. Also cover the chimney with fabric. Glue in place as shown.

11

12

11. Trim the backs of the trees and glue in place. See the pattern and glue the leaves as shown. Then glue some cloth flowers on the grass and a bunch at each corner.

12. For the nosegay: wrap the flower ends with floral tape. Then wind the end around a nail to curl. Glue the flowers between the leaves. With the pink and blue ribbon, tie a bow and glue onto the nosegay. Trim the ends.

GOOD MORNING

YOU WILL NEED:

5"x6 1/2" lightweight & heavyweight cardboards
5"x6 1/2" thermolam or needlepunch
6"x7" fabric for background
2" wide mirror
30" of 3/4" wide flat white lace
21" of 1/8" wide burgundy ribbon
28" of single fold bias tape
paint or pens for saying (see introduction)
transfer pencil
craft glue or glue gun

1 **2**

1. Trace the oval pattern on page 7 and cut out of heavyweight and lightweight cardboards. Follow steps 2 thru 6, on pages 1 and 2, to cover the heavyweight oval and make the saying.

2. Run a bead of glue along the edge of the oval. Attach one end of the bias and tightly pull as you go around the oval. Overlap the ends and glue down.

3  **4**

3. Run a bead of glue along the edge of the mirror and attach the bias tape as above. Glue the mirror to the oval.

4. Run a bead of glue on the back of the oval and attach the lace, gathering as you go. Cut a 9" piece of ribbon and glue in place for the hanger. Glue the lightweight oval to the back. Make a bow out of the remaining ribbon and glue above the mirror. Tack down each ribbon tail with a drop of glue.

HOME IS WHERE THE  IS

YOU WILL NEED:

6"x7" lightweight & heavyweight cardboards
7"x8" fabric (background)
2"x33" fabric (ruffle)
6"x7" thermolam or needlepunch
2"x7" piece of Aida cloth, 14 count
magenta & blue embroidery floss
cross-stitch needle & sewing needle
18" of 1/8" wide blue ribbon
Fray Check ™ (found in fabric stores)
heavy craft glue or glue gun

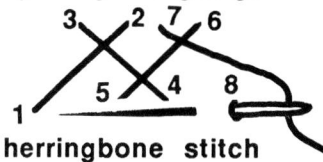
herringbone stitch

1. Match the center dot on the saying (see inside back cover) to the center of the Aida cloth. Work the cross stitch using two strands of floss. Run a line of Fray Check™ along each side of the saying, two squares from the stitching. Let dry and cut the cloth two squares from the stitching on each long side.

2. Trace the heart pattern on page 7. Cut out of heavyweight and lightweight cardboard. Glue the thermolam to the heavyweight heart and trim to fit. Follow steps 2 thru 4, on page 1, to cover the heart.

3. Position the saying on the heart and glue down. With two strands of magenta floss, embroider along each side of the saying using a herringbone stitch. Then sew a running stitch as shown on the pattern.

4. Fold the fabric strip in half lengthwise, wrong sides together and sew a running stitch along the raw edges. Run a bead of glue on the back of the heart and attach the ruffle, gathering as you go. Cut the ribbon in half. Tie a bow in one half, set aside. Glue two ends to the heart as shown. Glue the bow to the center of the ribbon. Glue the lightweight cardboard in place.

1 2

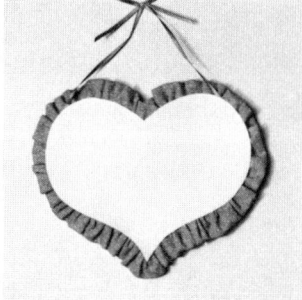

3 4

POCKET BASKET

YOU WILL NEED:

10" square blue calico fabric
5"x10" thermolam or needlepunch
2"x6" Aida cloth, 14 count
cross stitch needle & sewing needle
sewing thread to match fabric
50" of 1/8" wide blue ribbon
blue embroidery thread
dried flowers
craft glue

1

2

3

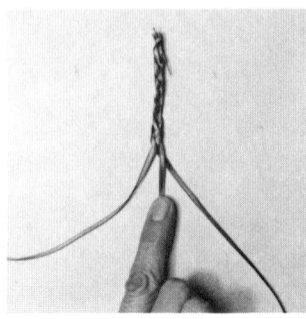

4

1. Match the center dot on the saying (see inside back cover) to the center of the Aida cloth. Work the cross stitch using two strands of floss. Trace the heart pattern on page 7. Cut out 4 hearts from fabric and 2 from thermolam.

2. Cut one heart in half along the cutting line shown on the pattern. Fold each cut edge under 1/2". Place each folded edge on the Aida cloth two squares away from the stitching. Machine sew along each folded edge. Trim the Aida cloth to match the heart shape.

3. Place the cross stitch heart on top of the thermolam, right side up. Then lay another heart right side down. Machine stitch the three layers together. Use a 1/4" seam allowance and leave an opening. Clip the curves and turn right side out. Hand sew the opening closed. Repeat for the other heart.

4. Beginning at the top of the Aida cloth, hand sew the hearts together. For the handle: braid three 12" lengths of ribbon. Knot each end to hold the braid and glue to the basket. Make two bows and glue over the braided ends. Break off 3" long lengths of dried flowers, dip the ends in glue and insert in the basket.

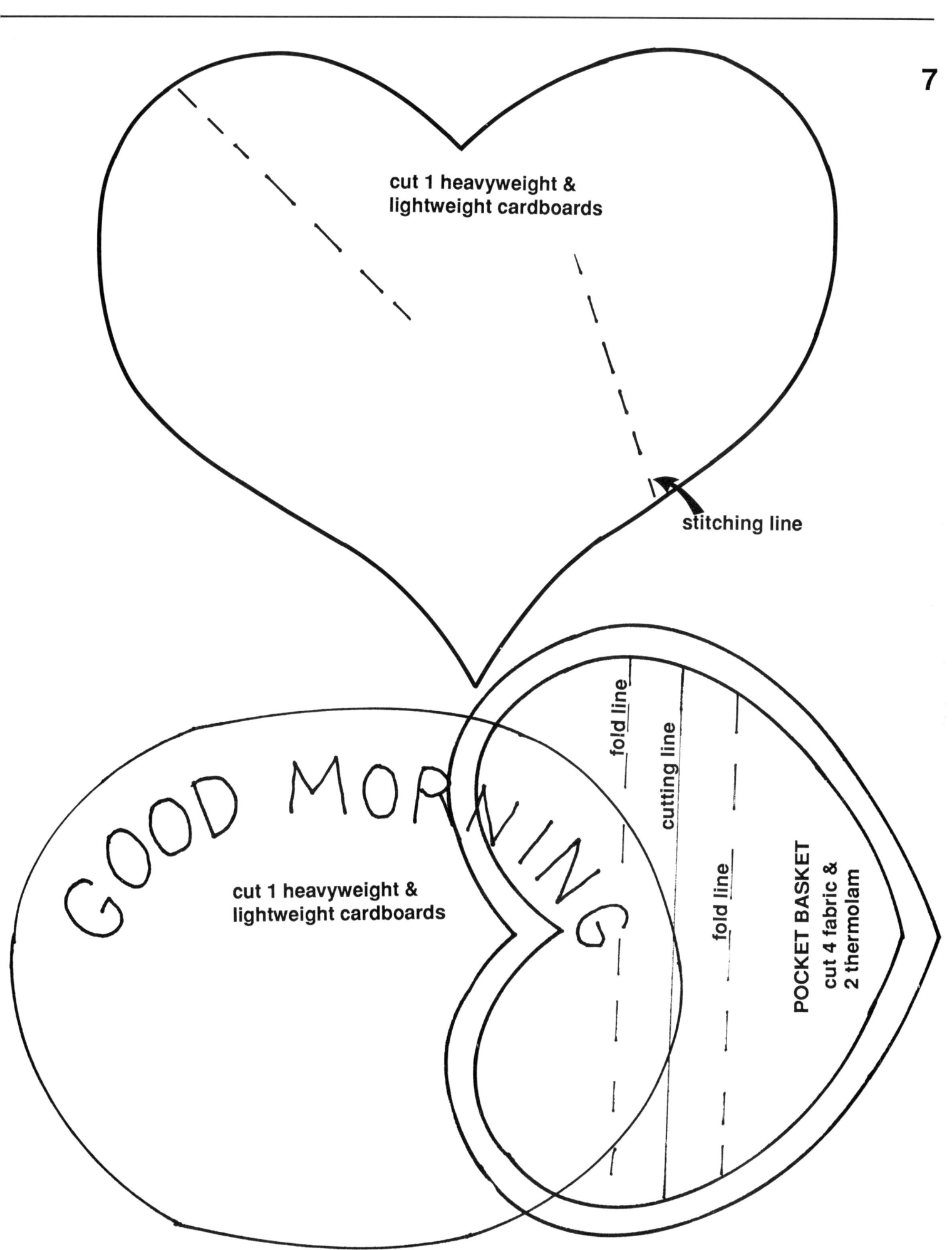

HOME SWEET HOME

YOU WILL NEED:

7"x7" lightweight & heavyweight cardboards
5"x6 1/2" pindot fabric (house)
3"x3" gingham (chimney)
5"x7 1/2" calico (roof, doors & windows)
scrap fabric (flower boxes & door window)
7"x7" thermolam or needlepunch
12 1/2" of 1/16" wide white ribbon
7 1/2" of 1/8" wide white ribbon
paint or pens for saying (see introduction)
6 cloth flowers
1 pink seed bead (doorknob)
craft glue or glue gun

1   Trace the patterns on page 9 onto paper. Cut the house and roof out of heavyweight and lightweight cardboards. Glue thermolam to the house and roof, trim to fit. Follow steps 2 thru 6, on pages 1 and 2, to cover the pieces and make the saying. Be sure to cover the chimneys with the gingham.

2   Glue the lightweight cardboard pieces to the backs of the house and roof. Glue the roof in place. For the hanger: cut off a 2" length of 1/4" wide ribbon and glue on the back.

3   Cut the door and windows out of the appropriate fabrics. Glue to the house. Glue 1/8" wide ribbon around the door. Outline the tops, sides and panes on the windows with 1/16" wide ribbon.

4   Cut the door window and flower boxes out of lightweight cardboard. Cover with fabric but don't use thermolam. Wrap thread around the door window. Glue in place. Add flowers and the doorknob.

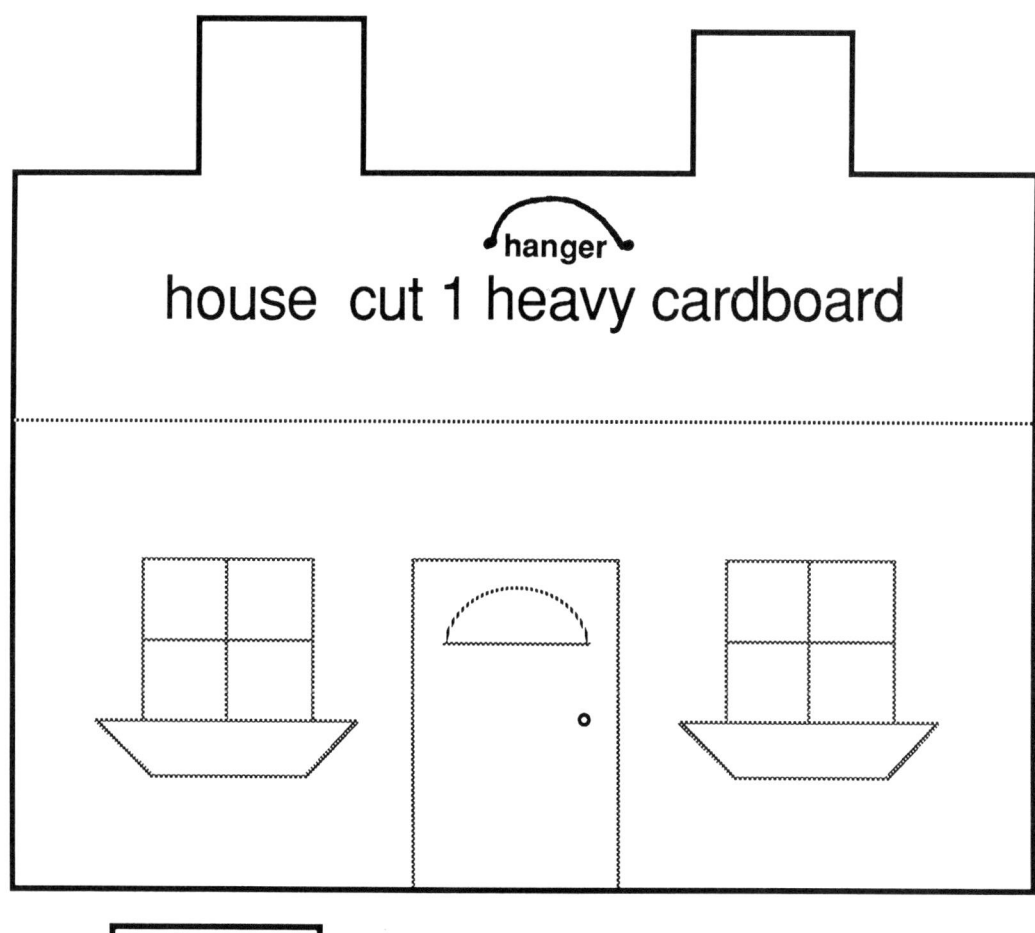

HOME IS WHERE YOU HANG YOUR HEART

YOU WILL NEED:

9" square heavyweight and lightweight cardboards
9 1/4" square fabric (circle)
2"x54" fabric (ruffle)
3" square fabric (doors & windows)
4" square fabric (house)
2 1/2"x4 1/2" fabric (roof)
9" square thermolam or needlepunch
1" square red felt (heart)
1 white pearl seed bead (doorknob)
heavy white sewing thread
potpourri
12" of 1/8" wide brown ribbon
paint or pens for saying (see introduction)
craft glue or glue gun

1

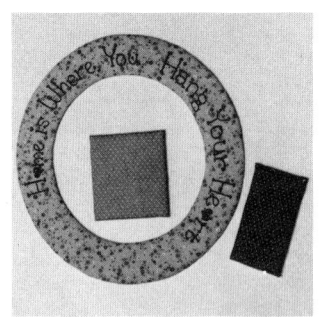

2

1. Trace the patterns on page 11 onto paper. Cut them out of the appropriate cardboards and thermolam as indicated on each pattern. Glue the thermolam to the circle, house and roof. Trim to fit.

2. Follow steps 2 thru 6, on pages 1 and 2, to cover the pieces and make the saying.

3

4

3. Glue the lightweight cardboards to the back of the house and roof. Then glue the roof to the house as shown, see the pattern for placement.

4. Cover the doors and windows with fabric. Wrap the windows with heavy sewing thread and glue in place. Glue on the door and add the seed bead for a doorknob. Cut the small heart out of red felt and glue above the door.

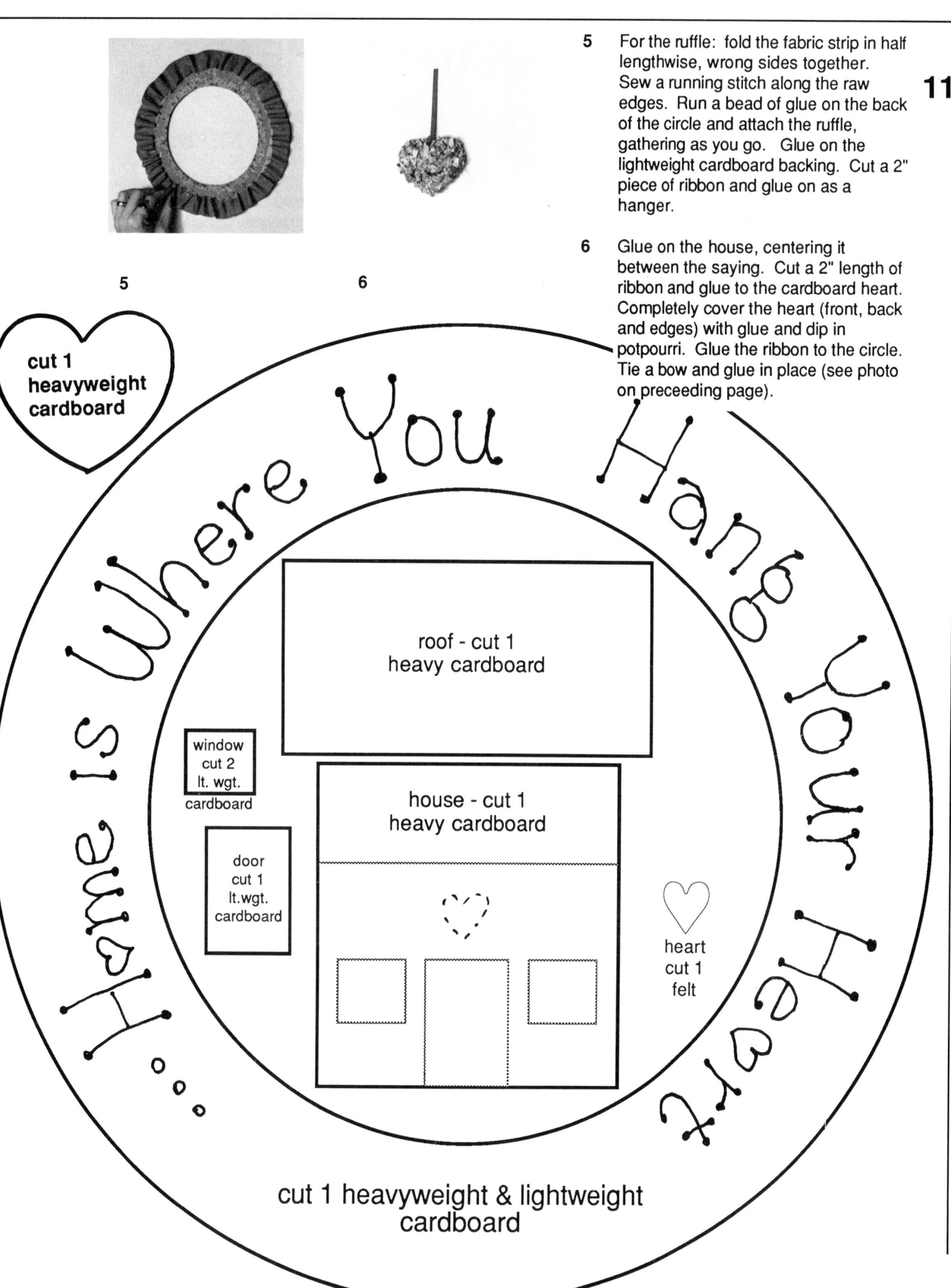

5. For the ruffle: fold the fabric strip in half lengthwise, wrong sides together. Sew a running stitch along the raw edges. Run a bead of glue on the back of the circle and attach the ruffle, gathering as you go. Glue on the lightweight cardboard backing. Cut a 2" piece of ribbon and glue on as a hanger.

6. Glue on the house, centering it between the saying. Cut a 2" length of ribbon and glue to the cardboard heart. Completely cover the heart (front, back and edges) with glue and dip in potpourri. Glue the ribbon to the circle. Tie a bow and glue in place (see photo on preceeding page).

ENTER WITH HAPPY HEART

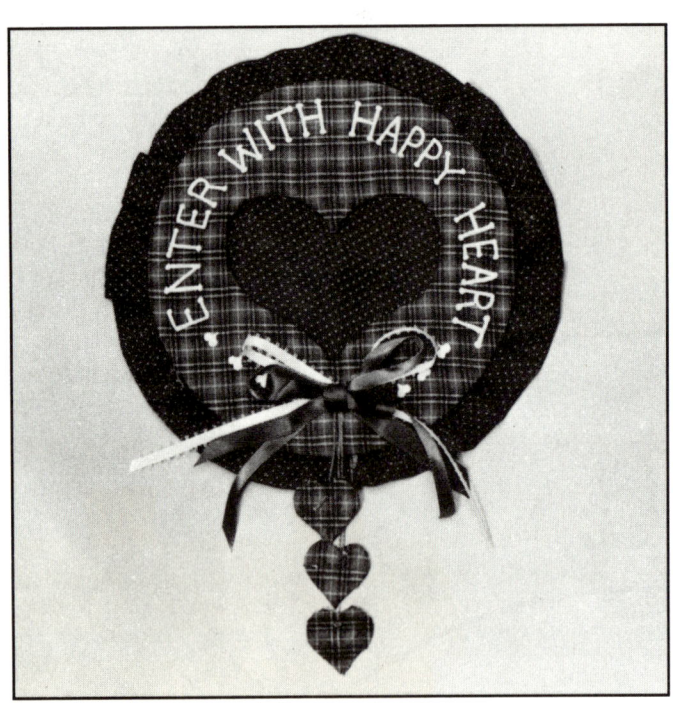

YOU WILL NEED:

7"x8" heavyweight and lightweight cardboards
7 1/2" square fabric (background)
2 1/2"x42" fabric (ruffle)
5" square fabric (heart)
7" square thermolam or needlepunch
22" of 1/2" wide blue ribbon
22" of 1/4" wide blue ribbon
22" of 1/4" white feather-edge ribbon
paint or pens for saying (see introduction)
blue pearl cotton or crochet thread
large eyed sewing needle
craft glue or glue gun

1

2

3    4

1. Trace the patterns on page 17 onto paper. Cut the circle out of lightweight and heavyweight cardboards, then cut the center heart from the heavyweight circle only. Cut 3 smaller hearts from the lightweight cardboard. Glue the thermolam on the heavyweight circle and trim to fit, be sure to cut out the center heart.

2. Cover the circle and make the saying by following steps 2 thru 6, on pages 1 and 2.

3. For the ruffle: fold the fabric strip in half lengthwise, wrong sides together. Sew a running stitch along the raw edges. Run a bead of glue on the back of the circle and attach the ruffle, gathering as you go.

4. Lightly glue the 5" square fabric to the center of the lightweight cardboard circle. Then glue to the back of the heavyweight circle. Cut a 2" length of 1/4" wide blue ribbon and glue for a hanger.

"Happiness is Homemade" design shown cut out of wood and (below) cross stitched.

"Home Sweet Home" is created in wood. Then, with another saying, it is made over cardboard and, finally, in a hoop with quilting.

14

Here the "Welcome Friends" design becomes a Christmas scene. Then with the goose pattern below, it takes on another look.

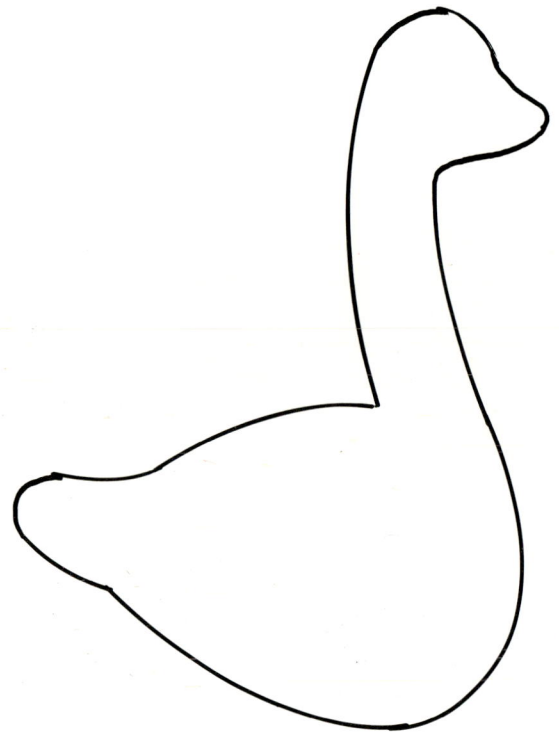

The "Joy Bird" is ready for Christmas.

The goose pattern (above) in the circle pattern from page 11.

This heart pattern is cross stitched and added to a bunch of dried flowers. Then it is made as a package tie. (The heart is also in the window on the cover of this book).

15

In this applique the heart is stuffed.

A piece of cross stitch can find a home in many places, like this pillow.

16

Another "Pocket Basket." The cross stitch pattern is inside the back cover.

The "Slate" stencil is made on a shaker box.

"Enter With Happy Heart" is painted on wood.

"Good Morning" takes on two new looks.

5. Cover the three hearts with fabric as you did in step 2 (no thermolam is used). Then glue the back of each heart to a piece of fabric. Trim to fit.

6. Thread the large eyed needle with the pearl cotton, tie a knot in one end. Insert the needle into a heart as shown, leave 3" of pearl cotton hanging. Repeat for the other hearts. Glue to the circle as shown in the photo on the preceding page.

7. Tie a shoestring bow in each length of ribbon. Glue to the circle as shown, one on top of the other. Trim each ribbon tail at an angle.

cut 3 lightweight cardboard

ENTER WITH HAPPY HEART

cut out heart

cut 1 circle of heavyweight & lightweight cardboards

JOY BIRD

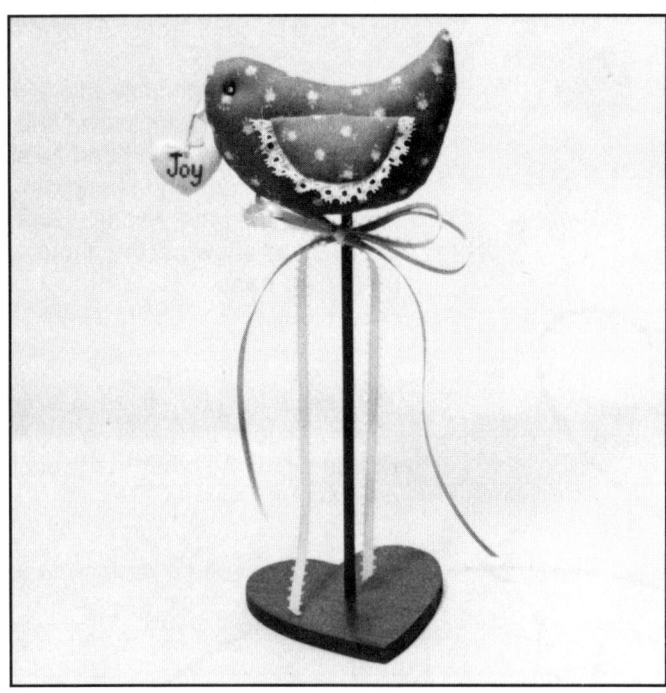

YOU WILL NEED:

6"x8" fabric (bird)
10" of 1/2" wide gathered white lace
2" of 3/8" wide ribbon (beak)
24" of 1/8" wide rose ribbon
24" of 1/4" wide lt. green feather-edge ribbon
polyester fiberfill stuffing
2"x4" Hardanger cross stitch fabric
rose embroidery thread
cross stitch needle
2 black sequins
2 pink seed beads
10" of pink pearl cotton
needle and pink sewing thread
8" length of 1/4" wooden dowel
optional: 4" long heart, circle or square block of wood with 1/4" hole drilled in the center
paint for the dowel and wood
craft glue

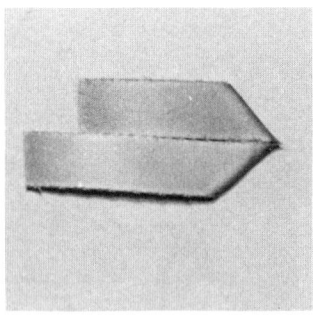
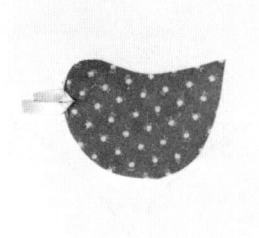

1 2

1. Trace the bird and wing patterns from page 20 onto paper. Cut out of fabric. For the beak: fold the ribbon as shown forming a triangle and glue to hold the ends down.

2. With the fabric facing you, position the beak as shown. Pin in place. Put the bird patterns together, right sides together. Using a 1/4" seam allowance, machine stitch around the entire body.

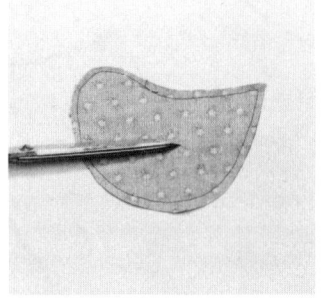
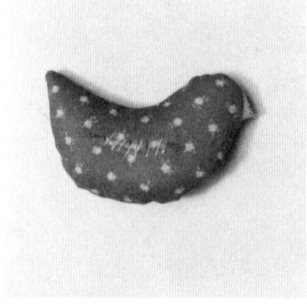

3 4

3. Trim the seams and clip the curves. Cut a short slit on one side of the body, see the pattern for placement. Turn right side out.

4. Firmly stuff and slip stitch the slit closed.

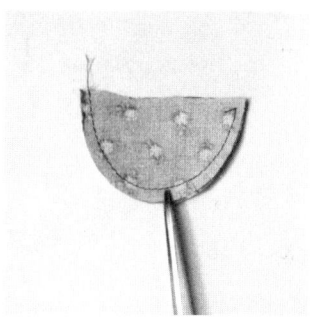
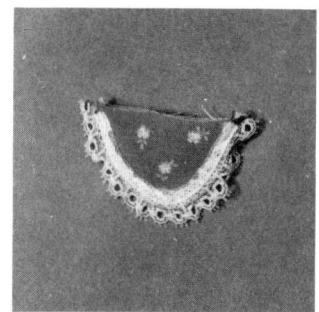

5

6

5. For one wing: take two wing pieces, with right sides together machine stitch the curved edge. Clip the curves and turn the wing right side out.

6. Run a bead of glue along the curved edge and attach the lace. Repeat steps 5 and 6 for the other wing.

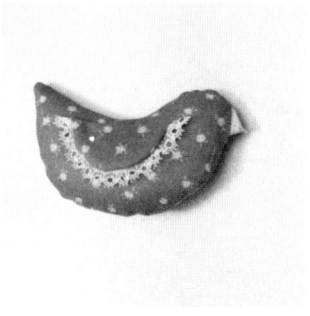

7

8

7. When the glue is dry, fold the raw edges under and glue the wings to the sides of the bird. Be sure one wing covers the slit on the body.

8. For the eyes: use double thread knotted in a needle. Insert at the eye placement, come out at other eye placement. Slip on a sequin and bead. Put the needle back through the sequin and stitch thru the bird. Have the needle come out at the other eye placement. Repeat for the other eye. Tie off.

9

10

9. Paint the wooden base and dowel. Let dry. Cut the cross stitch fabric in half making two 2" squares. See the JOY pattern inside the back cover. With one strand of thread work the JOY in the center of one square. Trace the heart pattern on page 20 and cut two hearts from the cross stitch fabric--be sure to center the JOY on one heart.

10. Run a fine bead of glue around each heart shape. Let dry. Put right sides together and machine stitch, leaving an opening. Clip the curves, turn right side out and stuff. Close the opening by hand stitching.

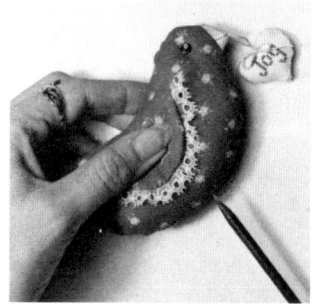

11

12

11. Thread a needle with pearl cotton, string the cross stitch heart and thread through the beak, tie the ends in a bow.

12. Sharpen one end of the dowel in a pencil sharpener. Carefully work into the bird then remove. Dip the end of the dowel in glue and re-insert. Lay the ribbons together and tie around the dowel, make a bow. Glue the dowel into the wooden base.

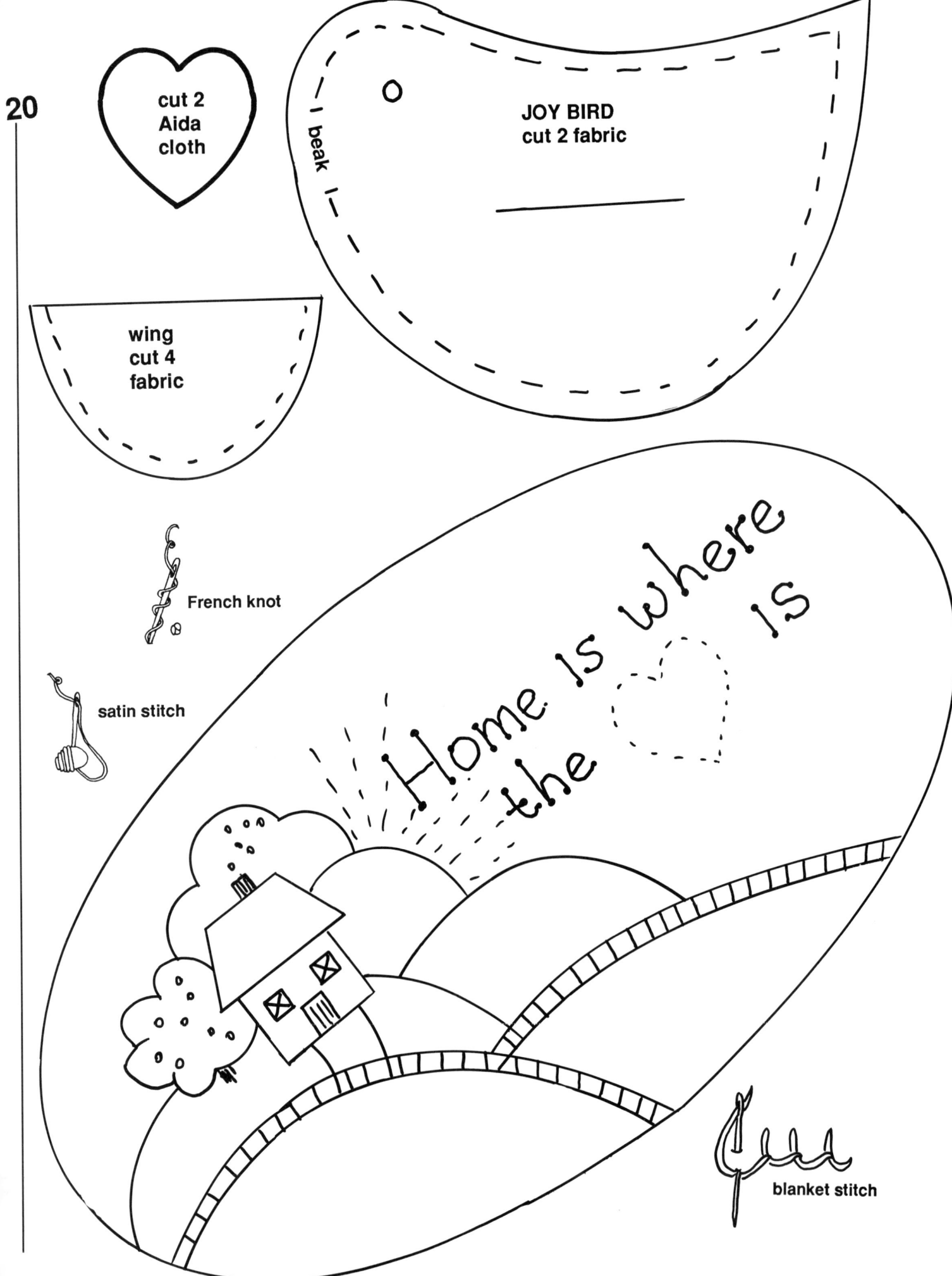

HOME IS WHERE THE HEART IS

YOU WILL NEED:

2 1/2"x48" fabric (ruffle)
7"x12" pindot fabric (background)
scraps of co-ordinating fabrics
thread to match each fabric
4"x9" embroidery hoop
embroidery thread & needle
24" of 1/8" wide ribbon
24" of 1/4" wide ribbon
1 1/2" square lightweight cardboard
paint or pens for saying (see introduction)
dressmakers carbon paper
typing paper
fabric glue
craft glue or glue gun

1 2

3 4

1. Trace the pattern on page 20 and pattern pieces on page 22 onto paper. Position the complete pattern on the background fabric. Slip the carbon paper under the pattern and trace around the cloud and hills. This will help in positioning. Also trace the saying.

2. Tape the background fabric to a piece of cardboard and make the saying.

3. Cut the pattern pieces out of the various fabrics. Dab the fabric glue on the back of the cloud #1 and place on the background fabric. Continue positioning each piece using the fabric glue and the carbon drawing. Work in order from #2 thru #10.

4. Set your sewing machine to a very close zig zag stitch, 1/8" wide. Slip the applique onto the typing paper. Using thread to match, sew around each pattern piece in the order in which they were placed. In some places it may be necessary to fold back an adjacent pattern piece to hide the beginning or ending of your stitching.

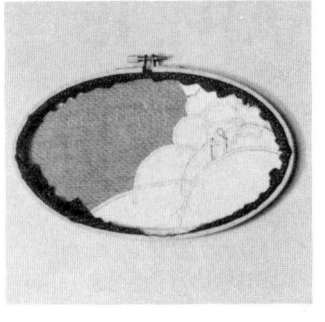

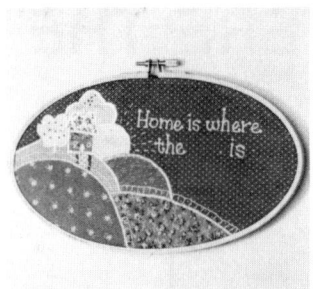

5

Home is where
the is

6

Home is where
the is

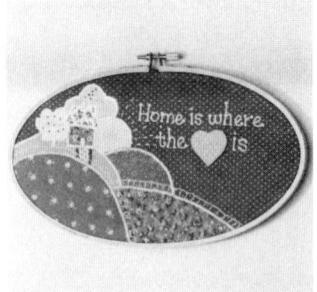

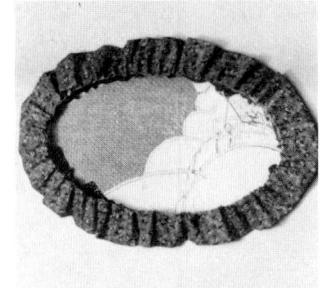

7

8

5 Remove the excess typing paper. Center the fabric in the hoop. Pull the fabric taut as you tighten the screw. Trim to 1/2" beyond the hoop and glue the excess fabric to the inside of the hoop.

6 Embroidery stitches: with 2 strands of embroidery floss make satin stitches for the tree trunk, chimney and front door. Use French knots for the fruit on the tree and chimney smoke. Use straight stitches for the sun's rays and windows. And a blanket stitch for the fences.

7 Trace the heart and cut it out of lightweight cardboard. Cover with fabric, see page 1, steps 3 and 4. Glue to the applique.

8 For the ruffle: fold the fabric strip in half lengthwise, wrong sides together. Sew a running stitch along the raw edges. Run a bead of glue on the back of the hoop and attach the ruffle, gathering as you go. Lay the ribbons together and tie a shoestring bow. Glue to the hoop.

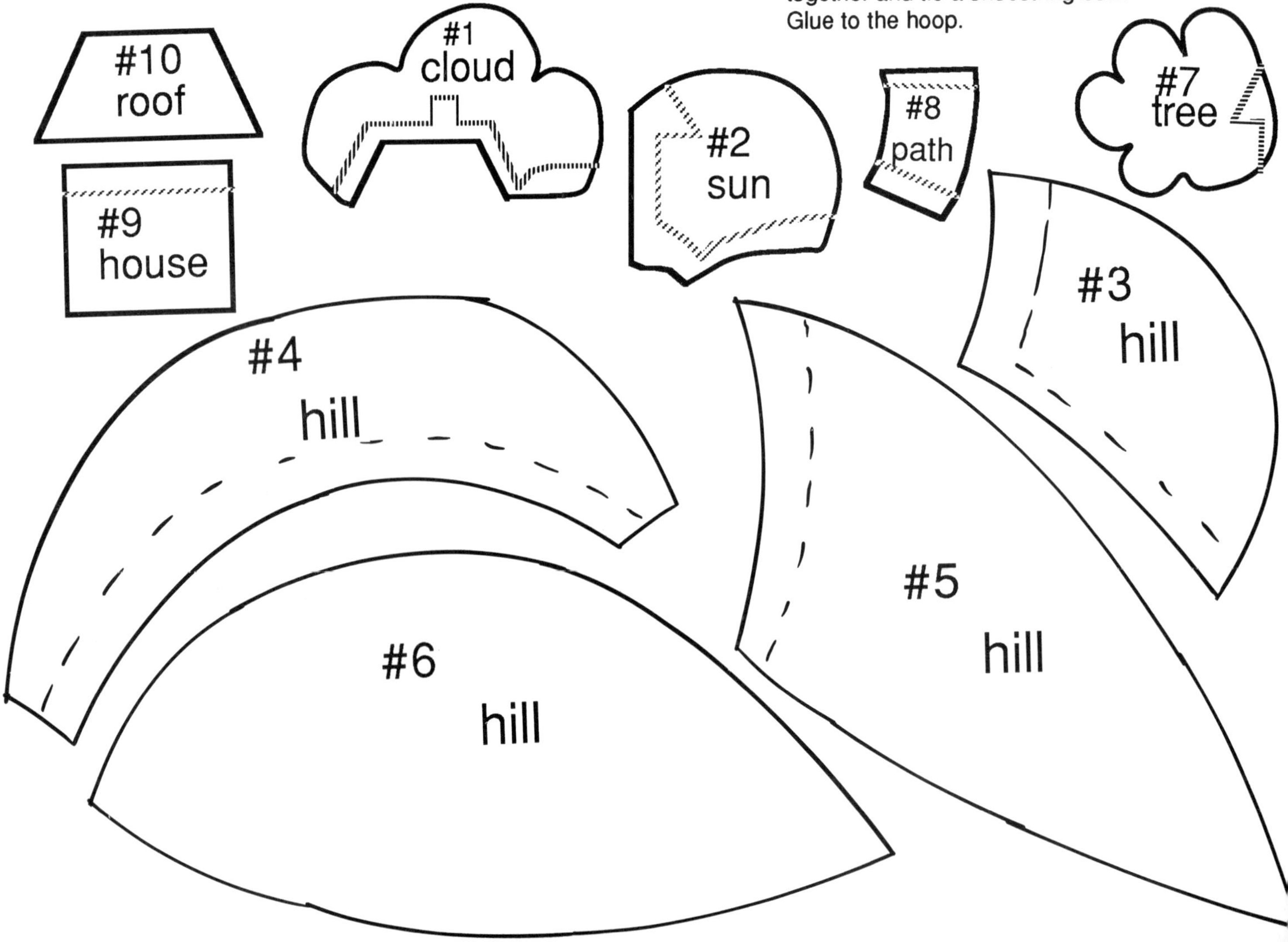

#10 roof
#1 cloud
#2 sun
#8 path
#7 tree
#9 house
#3 hill
#4 hill
#5 hill
#6 hill

HAPPINESS IS HOMEMADE

YOU WILL NEED:

4 3/4"x5 3/4" fabric (background)
6 1/2"x7 1/2" fabric (backing)
1 1/2"x24" fabric (border)
1 1/2"x7" fabric (corners)
3"x4" fabric (house)
4"x7" fabric (roof, windows & door)
3 1/2" square fabric (hangers), cut in half
6 1/2"x7 1/2" thermolam or needlepunch
paint or pens for saying (see introduction)
sewing thread to match fabrics
1/4" wooden dowel, 7" long
2 beads to fit 1/4" dowel
fabric glue and craft glue

1

2

1. Trace the pattern pieces on page 24 and cut out of the appropriate fabrics. Position them on the background fabric using the fabric glue to hold the pieces in place.

2. Set your sewing machine to a very close zig zag stitch, 1/8" wide. Slide the applique onto the typing paper and sew around each pattern piece using matching thread. Remove the excess typing paper.

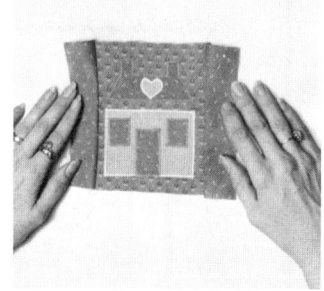

3

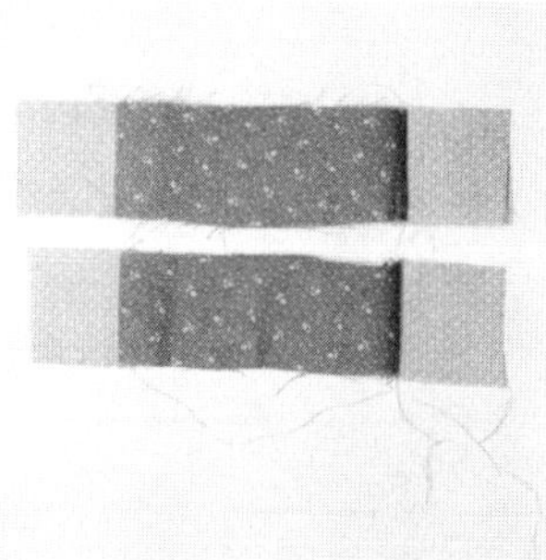

4

3. Cut 2 pieces of the border fabric each 5 3/4" long. Sew to each side of the applique using a 1/4" seam allowance.

4. Cut 2 pieces of the border fabric each 4 3/4" long. Cut 4 pieces of the corner fabric, each 1 1/2" long. Sew a corner piece to each end of the border fabric using a 1/4" seam allowance. Iron all seams flat.

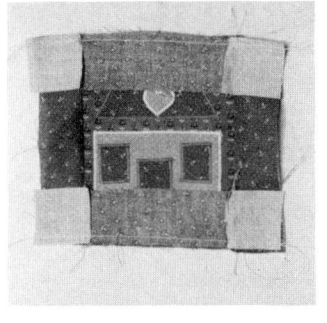 

5   6

 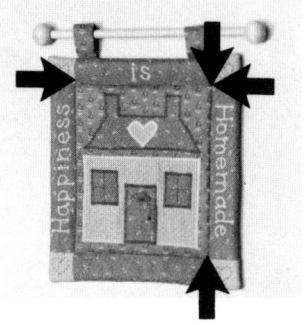

7   8

5. Sew the strips to each end of the applique, right sides together using a 1/4" seam allowance.

6. For each hanger: fold the fabric in half lengthwise, right sides together. Stitch along one long edge using a 1/4" seam allowance. Turn right side out. Fold in half and place as shown. Pin to hold.

7. Place the applique right side up on the thermolam. Add the backing right side down. Stitch all the way around leaving an opening. Clip the corners, turn right side out. Close the opening by hand stitching.

8. Stitch around the background fabric (stitch in the seam, see the arrows). With sewing thread make the hearts at each corner, the panes in the windows, the window in the door and the doorknob. Carefully use paints or pens to make the saying, see the introduction. Glue the beads to the ends of the dowel and hang.

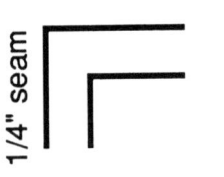

quilted corner heart

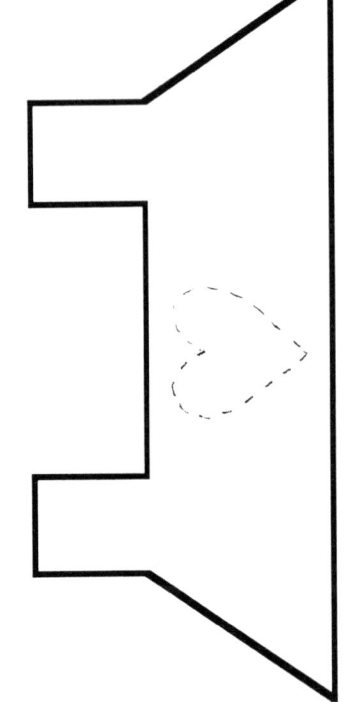

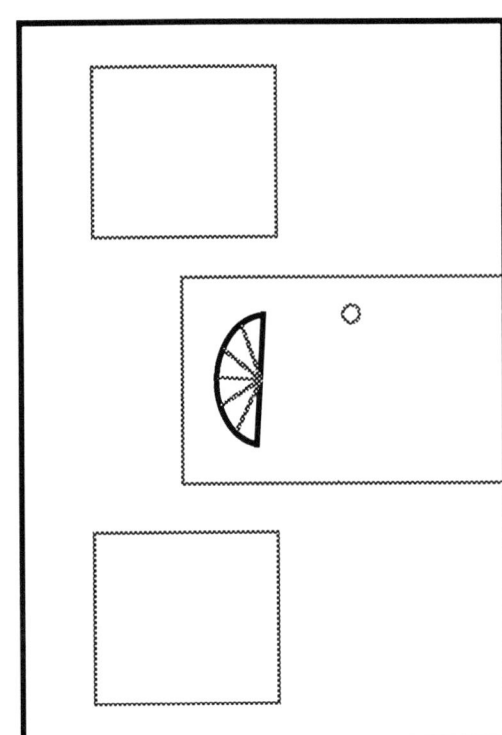

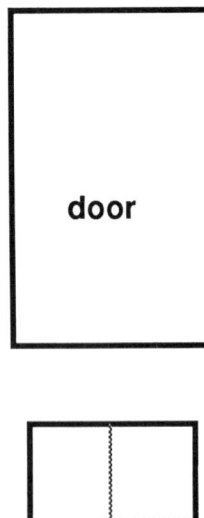

door

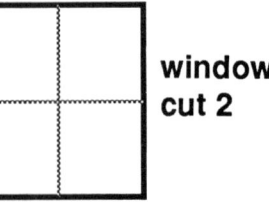

window
cut 2

SLATE

YOU WILL NEED:

6"x8" slate
sheet of stencil paper or mylar
stain
x-acto knife
piece of glass (perhaps from a picture frame)
water base varnish
three 3/8" stencil brushes
#0 liner brush
stencil or acrylic paints--lt. blue, white, brown, rust, dark green, gold, red
carbon paper & ball point pen
paint or pens for saying (see introduction)
sawtooth hanger

1

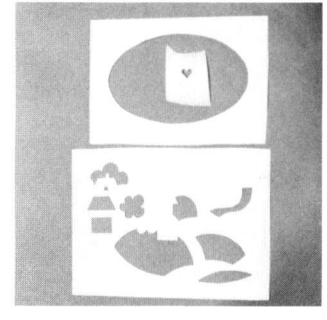

2

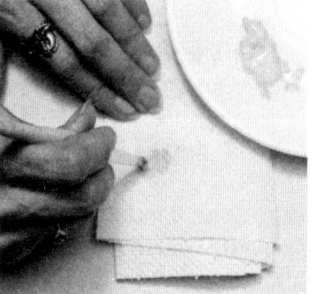

3

4

1 Stain the slate frame. Trace the saying from page 27 onto paper. Position it on the slate and slip a piece of carbon paper under it. With a ball point pen trace the saying onto the slate then make the saying. Use acrylics for the hearts and house on the frame (cut a stencil pattern for the heart).

2 Trace the stencil pattern and oval onto paper. Place a piece of glass over the pattern. Tape the mylar to the glass and cut out the oval with an x-acto knife. Then re-position the mylar and cut out each shape.

3 Tape the mylar oval to the center of the slate. Stir or shake the paint and pour out a small amount of lt. blue. Dip only the tip of the brush in the paint. Because you want a "dry" brush, dab the brush on a folded paper towel to remove any excess paint.

4 Hold the brush straight up and use a tapping motion to fill the oval. Work from the outside edge toward the center. It will take 2 coats to cover the slate with lt. blue but it is not necessary to cover the entire oval with paint. Wipe the brush thoroughly with a paper towel.

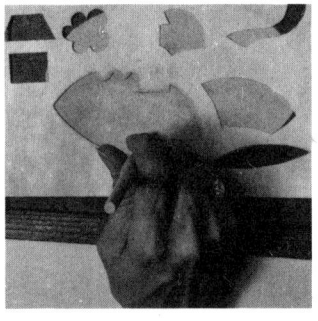

5

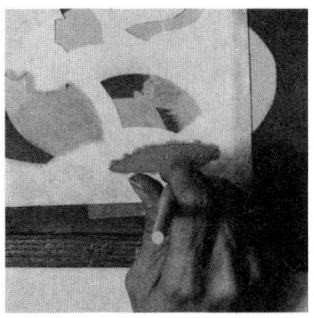

6

5 Add some dark green paint to white paint to get a light green. Position the front hill #1 and stencil.

6 Add a little more green for a darker shade and position hill #2, stencil.

7

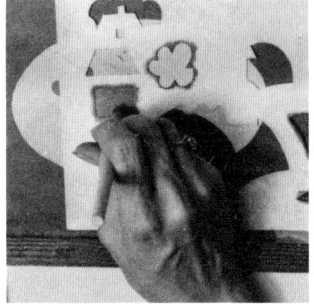

8

7 Hill #3 is all dark green, stencil it. Place the tree #4 and stencil with dark green.

8 Wipe the brush well and do the house with rust paint. Wipe the brush again and do the roof with brown. Use rust again for the chimney.

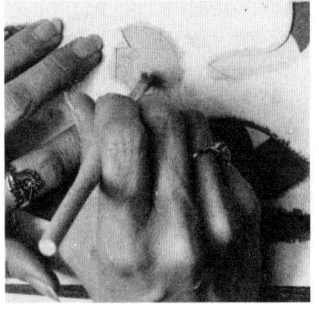

9

10

9 Add brown to the white and do the path. Wipe the brush thoroughly and do the gold sun.

10 With a clean brush make the white cloud.

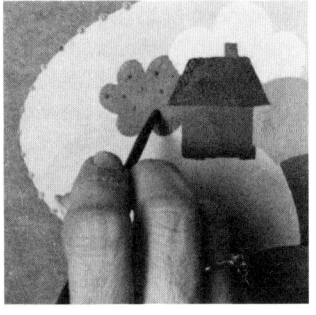

11

12

11 Dip the end of a wooden paint brush into gold paint and touch to the slate to make the dots around the oval. Make red dots for the apples in the tree.

12 The fences, door, windows and sun's rays are painted with the liner brush. Let dry and varnish only the wooden frame and the stenciled area, not the slate. Nail on the hanger.

The path to a friend's house is never long

27

WELCOME

YOU WILL NEED:

Two pieces of 3"x16" muslin
sewing thread
28" of 3/4" wide flat lace
29" of 1/8" wide lt. blue ribbon
heavy sewing thread or dental floss
lt. blue and rust dried flowers
1/2"x2" piece of cardboard
large jingle bell
1" stencil letters
two 1/2" stencil brushes
stencil or acrylic paint--lt. blue and rust
craft glue

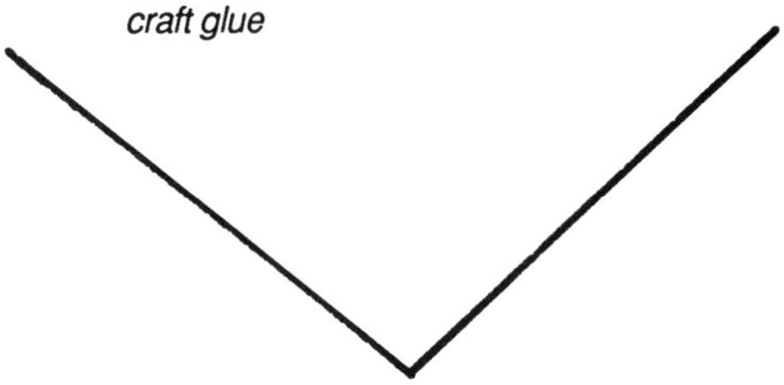

1

2

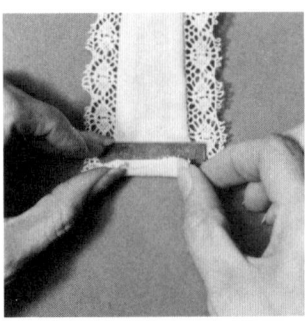

3

4

1. Tape one of the muslin strips to a flat surface. Insert a folded paper towel under the muslin. Measure 2 1/2" from the top and stencil a rust heart, see stencil directions on page 25, steps 3 and 4. Measure 1/2" from the bottom of the heart, stencil a "W." The letters are 1/4" apart. Finish with another rust heart.

2. Fold under the long edges of each muslin strip 1/2", press. Following the pattern above, cut a point at the end of each muslin strip. Turn the fabric under, press and pin to hold.

3. Place the stenciled strip on the table. Cut the lace in half making two 14" pieces. Lay a piece on each side of the muslin. Place the other muslin strip on top and sew along both long edges and the point.

4. Glue the cardboard 1/4" from the top. Fold the muslin over as shown, glue down. Then fold over again and glue. Attach a 10" length of ribbon for the hanger. Use heavy thread or floss to sew on the bell. Glue the flowers to the top. Make two bows and glue as shown.